S0-AXM-364

WITHDRAWN

MAR -- 2013

Catfish, Cod, Salmon, and Scrod

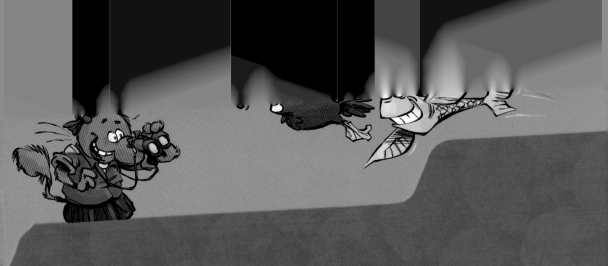

For my friends at St. Christopher
School in Rocky River, Ohio
—B.P.C.

To Mathilde Milot, my son's godmother.
The best one in the whole world
—M.G.

Fish:
an animal that
lives its entire
life in water
and has a
backbone

Catfish, Cod, Salmon, and Scrod

What Is a Fish?

by Brian P. Cleary

illustrations by Martin Goneau

DES PLAINES PUBLIC LIBRARY
1501 ELLINWOOD STREET
DES PLAINES, IL 60016

M Millbrook Press • Minneapolis

What's a type of animal that swims both day and night

and lives beneath the water?

If you guessed a **fish**, you're right!

Fish can use their gills to breathe, and all of them have tails—

also fins to help them steer

and most of them have scales.

Fish are vertebrates, which means that they all have a spine—

a built-in kind of backbone
that is part of their design.

Most **fish** are cold-blooded, so their temperature conforms

to that of their surroundings—
whether cool or hot or warm.

Some are spotted.

Some are striped.

Some are multicolor.

Some are bright and beautiful.

And some? A little duller.

Can you name a type of **fish?**

There's catfish,

carp,

and cod,

marlin,

mackerel,

man-of-war.

There's salmon,
shark, and scrod.

Piranhas are another fish, and if you were to get one,

you'd watch it and you'd feed it,
but you wouldn't want to pet one!

The stingray and the guppy
are among the very few

that don't lay eggs but give live birth
when adding to their crew.

Some **fish** live in oceans.

And others? Streams and lakes.

Some share their homes with humpback whales,

and some with ducks and drakes.

Some eat plants, like seaweed,
while some eat other fishes.

A few eat bugs and plankton,
and they find them both delicious.

Some are smaller than your thumb.
Still other **fish** can grow

to be about the size of
two big trucks parked in a row.

Some **fish** walk a bit on land,
and others briefly fly.

Using large pectoral fins,
they glide into the sky!

This book contains more fishy facts
in back, just look and see—

So if you're ever tested, then you'll pass it "swimmingly"!

So, what is a **fish**?
Do you know?

An animal is a fish if . . .
- it lives its entire life in water;
- it has a backbone
  (it's a vertebrate).

In addition, all fish . . .

- have gills;
- have fins.

And most fish . . .

- are born from eggs;
- have scales;
- are cold-blooded animals. This means they cannot make their own body heat. Their bodies are the same temperature as their surroundings.

Find activities, games, and more at
www.brianpcleary.com

ABOUT THE AUTHOR & ILLUSTRATOR

BRIAN P. CLEARY is the author of the Words Are CATegorical®, Math Is CATegorical®, Adventures in Memory™, Sounds Like Reading®, and Food Is CATegorical™ series, as well as several picture books and poetry books. He lives in Cleveland, Ohio.

MARTIN GONEAU is the illustrator of the Food Is CATegorical™ series. He lives in Trois-Rivières, Québec.

LERNER e SOURCE™

Expand learning beyond this printed book. Download free, complementary educational resources for this book from our website, www.lerneresource.com.

Text copyright © 2013 by Brian P. Cleary
Illustrations copyright © 2013 by Lerner Publishing Group, Inc.

All rights reserved. International copyright secured. No part of this book may be reproduced, stored in a retrieval system, or transmitted in any form or by any means—electronic, mechanical, photocopying, recording, or otherwise—without the prior written permission of Lerner Publishing Group, Inc., except for the inclusion of brief quotations in an acknowledged review.

Millbrook Press
A division of Lerner Publishing Group, Inc.
241 First Avenue North
Minneapolis, MN 55401 U.S.A.

Website address: www.lernerbooks.com

Fish Scale Background: © iStockphoto.com/Temmuz Can Arsiray.

Main body text set in Chauncy Decaf Medium 35/44. Typeface provided by the Chank Company.

Library of Congress Cataloging-in-Publication Data

Cleary, Brian P., 1959–
    Catfish, cod, salmon, and scrod : what is a fish? / by Brian P. Cleary ; illustrated by Martin Goneau.
        p.   cm. — (Animal groups are CATegorical)
    ISBN 978-0-7613-6211-1 (lib. bdg. : alk. paper)
    1. Fishes—Juvenile literature. I. Goneau, Martin, ill. II. Title.
    QL617.2.C54 2013
    597—dc23   2011050200

Manufactured in the United States of America
1 – DP – 7/15/2012